The EVENT Technique

The Business Side of Nonprofit Events

By Jill Kummer, Creator of the
EVENT Technique

The EVENT Technique
The Business Side of Nonprofit Events

Published by Geronimo Publishing, LLC
Allison Park, Pennsylvania

ISBN: 978-1-7339123-0-3

Cover design by Jim Saurbaugh, JS Graphic Design

doing business in the United States or any other jurisdiction, is the sole responsibility of the purchaser or reader.

Dedicated to the following:

Jordan, Branden, and Cameron ~ the reasons for everything.

My Mom and Dad who showed me it can be done and never to lose faith.

Kenton, founder of Blacktie, LLC, for giving me free rein to learn the event business from an entirely different perspective.

My business coach, Jim Palmer, who knew all along the potential of what I wanted to do while occasionally being the voice of doom.

Lastly, to Pete, who amongst other things taught me that there are six ways to grow a business and knew that I would try them all.

Your undying patience made it all worth it.

Table of Contents

Foreword

What could be more difficult than promoting and running a successful nonprofit event? How about writing a book on the topic and making it a bona fide page turner with nuggets of wisdom on every page!

That's exactly what Jill Kummer has done with *The EVENT Technique.*

I've known Jill for many years and have greatly admired her extensive career with Blacktie-Pittsburgh, a company she founded in the hospitality space, as well as her other entrepreneurial ventures such as EventsBurgh, Taste Great Wines, Taste Great Spirits, and Taste Great Beers.

As a business coach and author of several entrepreneurial books, I'm often asked to review books for clients and friends. When Jill asked me to review *The EVENT Technique*, I was happy to do it, but honestly, I braced myself for a long, tedious read. Wow, was I wrong!

Whether you are a veteran in the nonprofit space who's planned many fundraising events or just getting started, *The EVENT Technique* is a veritable goldmine of tried-and-true tips and strategies that can help those running events large and small do what those events are intended to do – raise funds rather than end up losing money!

I especially like the way Jill used the acronym, E.V.E.N.T. to describe exactly what it takes to have great success with your next event. At the end of each chapter, you'll find some handy summaries and action steps, all designed to take your next event to a higher, more profitable level.

Allow me to share just one of the nuggets you'll glean from *The EVENT Technique*: The second "E" in E.V.E.N.T. stands for Enthusiasm and Effort. As simple as this concept may seem, failure in this one critical area can doom even a well-attended event, and success always begins with enthusiasm and effort. What I really like is that on nearly every page, Jill gives you countless examples and tips on how to spot event-killing demons… and how to fix them, so they don't wreck your hard work and let your event finish with red ink.

If you're still not convinced that *The EVENT Technique* is a must read, then trust me, the bonus chapter on how to rock your events using the power of social media will do it. Jill shares some amazing tips on which social media platforms to use, what the right messaging should be, etc., and she also delves into the important (and current hot trend) of live streaming.

If you have any role in organizing, promoting, or running nonprofit events, do yourself a big favor and read *The EVENT Technique.* It will help you turn your next event into a profitable one and may even help make your job a little easier.

Jim Palmer –
The Dream Business Coach
www.GetJimPalmer.com

Foreword

Chapter One:

E: Evaluate

Ah, the fundraising event for the nonprofit organization – it can be a true boost to your mission… or the bane of your existence within your organization.

First things first. Let's be clear about what a nonprofit is. The name "nonprofit" can certainly be misleading. The inference may be that by its very nature it can't make money. Nothing could be further from the truth. Like any business, you must make money in order to carry out your mission and do the great work your organization was founded to do. The "nonprofit" reference means that no part of the organization's income is directed to members, directors, officers, etc. other than in the form of approved salaries. It's also defined as "a *business* granted tax-exempt status by the Internal Revenue Service."

Your organization is a business, and your organization needs money to function. So you appeal to donors and supporters for contributions, and then you decide to hold fundraising events to boost donations and income. "Fundraising events are a better way to ask for money," you say, "because donors are getting something in return. Besides, they're fun."

True and true… provided you plan and execute your event properly. Without the right planning and attention to the right details, your event can have the opposite effect – ending in the red with financial loss and a giant headache for everyone involved.

No matter the size of the event – from an open house at your facility to a lavish gala at the best venue in town – there are plenty of moving parts and places at which planning can fail, derailing your efforts to make money for your organization. This is exactly why I've created The EVENT Technique to provide a blueprint for you, so your event can and will be a great way to boost donations and revenue while having fun at the same time. We'll cover every aspect of the steps needed to really rock your event and ultimately further your organization's mission… why you do what you do.

So let's get started by evaluating where the money generated at any event comes from: donors and sponsors.

Your Donor Base

You already have a donor base – those people who contribute money to your nonprofit. The point of any fundraising event is to increase donations and awareness and in many cases, it is also the opportunity to provide your donors with an entertaining way to give more to your organization.

You must never take donors for granted! There are plenty of worthy organizations also vying for their donation dollars. Know your donors and why they support you. Obviously, donors believe in your mission or they would not have contributed dollar one. However, oftentimes, there is a story behind why they believe in your mission. For example, someone passed away from a particular disease, they love animals, maybe they were homeless at some point in their lives. Somewhere, somehow their life or an event in their life and your mission have intersected.

These are the people who are vital to get your message out about what your organization does and why it is beneficial. These people can make incredible inroads in communicating your message and mission, often with more impact than you can. Their stories will resonate, so when they appear, take the time to get to know them. Sit with them and discover their stories. Initially, it might be difficult for some people to open up about what transpired that brought them to your doorstep or motivated them to donate. However, once you develop a relationship with them, they can become, by far, your best ambassadors because they've probably lived through the issue that's at the heart of your mission.

Stories are impactful. What brought them to your nonprofit? Perhaps they first came to you for the support you offered when their life was disrupted and now they want to give back. Maybe it was a medical issue with a disease that needs much more research. Or a homelessness issue. Witnessing animals in need may have captured their attention. It's your job to discover their connection to you and their passion about what you do. Further your relationship with them by learning their story and asking them to contribute information as opposed to simply contributing dollars.

> **Evaluate why your donors support your organization.**

You have to understand donors' stories in order to evaluate their impact. And you have to evaluate their impact when determining whether to hold an event and what the event should be. Even though this is certainly a 10,000-foot view, all of this is intensely important.

The essence of maintaining your donor base is establishing, growing, and maintaining relationships. That said, donor relationships naturally ebb and flow. In the case of medical nonprofits in particular, some donors may be short-lived in the lifespan of the organization. For example, when someone passes away from a particular disease (leukemia, other cancers, ALS, Alzheimer's, etc.), there may be a number of one-time donors who contribute in the deceased's memory. Family members often initially come on board and donate because the organization helped them in their struggle with the disease and as they work through their grief. As months and years go by, they may not continue to contribute at the same pace or be as actively involved as they were. Their contributions and involvement may have been their method to process and move through their grief. Life has moved on and their attention is now elsewhere. They no longer feel compelled to support the organization. It happens. It's not a relationship that can or will continue.

Other donors remain for incredibly long periods of time, even to the point of leaving legacy contributions. In large part, the impetus for longevity is how they have been handled. People want to be recognized and appreciated. Introductory donors who have a story they want to share with others allows others to appreciate what they've been through. Long-standing donors and large contributors may be interested in serving not only as volunteers but on the board of directors. (A quick sidebar note: Do not think that you have to put every large donor on your board. Follow your governing guidelines when naming people to your board. Typically, the more people on the board, the less effective it becomes. Be very careful if you're choosing to put a donor on your board, regardless of their story.)

Not every donor wants recognition – public recognition. Hence, the anonymous category. Their

Recognize donors in the way they would like to be recognized.

reasons can vary from being highly personal to simply wanting to maintain anonymity. This doesn't mean you can ignore them. Quite the opposite. Consider hosting a donor appreciation event at no charge to the donor. Perhaps something very small and more intimate than your annual gala or similar event. It helps foster and strengthen your relationships with donors and will go a long way in furthering a consistent giving pattern and even legacy planning.

Everybody wants to be recognized for something. That is important to remember. It's really just being human, so never overlook or forget about the human side of donors and why they contribute to your organization.

Your Sponsors

In addition to individual donors, you must also consider and attract sponsors – local companies or national corporations that align with or believe in your mission.

Sponsorships are often a boon to any event, and failing to secure sponsorships can be a bust. These days, sponsorships are a brand new game. Potential sponsors are definitely looking for a return on their investment beyond corporate and community goodwill. How can you increase their return with your event? It matters, and sponsors need a tremendous amount of tender loving care (TLC). So how do you find and nurture sponsors?

First, you should personally visit the sponsor at their location. Often, it should be a small group of people from your organization actually sitting down with the deal maker of the company to get to know them, engage them, and get them involved. Again, it's about building a relationship. Invite them to visit you at your facility to fully understand the work you do and how you provide a benefit through your mission. You want to get them actively engaged and involved.

No one wants to support a "faceless" organization. Donors and sponsors aren't supporting the entity so much as they are supporting the people who do the work. Once you've established a relationship through visits, they'll have a face connected to the voice or behind the signature on a letter.

> **Sponsorships are really all about relationships.**

And it goes beyond creating the initial relationship. Once they're onboard, that relationship has to be nurtured. It's never enough to say to the company writing the check, "Thank you very much. We appreciate it, and we'll see you next year." There needs to be an ongoing, continual relationship with the company so that the company feels as though they are truly wanted and that their input is desired as well as having them make a monetary contribution. Never just take the check and run. The sponsor will never return to your organization again if you don't show them some TLC going forward and year-round.

There are a number of ways to reach sponsors and ensure their ROI is satisfactory. Right out of the box, schedule an interview with the CEO or decision maker – the person who's going to be the face of the company that is involved with your nonprofit. This person must fully understand what your organization does and why you matter.

Also, identify those in the sponsor company who can be tapped as ambassadors for your cause. These are the folks who can expand your reach tremendously. They may not be writing the check, but they'll make a commitment to your organization and will be able to also dedicate time and convey their passion to get their co-workers involved as well.

When you've secured a sponsor, you must clearly understand that it is no longer enough to put a company logo on event literature or as part of a PowerPoint presentation that runs in the background of the event. Companies expect far more, and there are plenty of other nonprofits chasing those donations. Truthfully, when you have a PowerPoint running during an event, take notice of how many people stand around watching it loop through. Pretty much no one. The message you send to your sponsors is essentially, "We appreciate that you're here and tonight's a special night, and we really won't talk to you again until this time next year." That certainly doesn't leave a good feeling with your sponsor.

The greater the level of sponsor donation the more TLC that company needs and should receive. You must continue to foster your relationship, so your sponsors stay onboard with you, not only for this event but for every event you have going forward. Your message needs to continually be: "We're grateful for your support, and we want you to see what your funding allows us to do throughout the year."

Along those lines, you should approach sponsors for other activities throughout the year, so your annual gala, for instance, doesn't come off as a one-trick-pony sort of event. Invite them to other events at no charge. For example, if a sponsor

> **Involve your sponsors throughout the year, not just at your main event.**

is underwriting a high-end gala, invite them to other smaller events at no charge throughout the year, so they can mingle and interact with your donor base, staff, and volunteers to really understand and become more involved with the grassroots side of your organization.

Be sure to spend time at the event introducing your sponsors to each other, a sort of ambassador-to-ambassador type relationship. As with so many other things in business, when looking for big dollars for an event, it's not necessarily what you know... it's who you know. Creating the ambassador-to-ambassador connection is a fabulous way to continue fostering those relationships because the companies are already likely working with each other in some way. Keeping sponsors engaged year-round is critical.

Handling sponsors and doling out the TLC takes time; however, it's well worth the investment. When done correctly, it benefits all parties. The challenge starts with determining who in your organization is going to contact and handle your sponsors. If it's a volunteer or board member, you must also create a way for them to report back on progress and details to keep the organization staff in the loop. Generally, more than one person should be paying attention to what the volunteer is doing in terms of soliciting and cultivating sponsors.

You'll want to target sponsors that logically fit your organization to begin with… companies that make sense. For example, if your nonprofit's mission is one that focuses on health or a particular disease, your targeting should start with hospitals and insurance companies, but don't stop there. Think about secondary or auxiliary industries. In this example, consider companies that supply wheelchairs or other medical supplies or other peripheral industries that dovetail into the main industry.

Keep in mind that not every company is a good fit. For example, of course you would not solicit a spirits company to provide the drinks at an event that is benefiting a rehab facility! You'd be surprised at how often these sorts of errors occur, and when they do, it's sayonara for both parties, and both organizations are particularly offended that that sponsor would have been solicited in the first place. Do a hard, 360-degree evaluation about who you are going to solicit for sponsors to be sure you can avoid these embarrassing mismatches.

Likewise, you ideally want sponsors who align with your nonprofit's goals and mission in some fashion. Chasing money for the sake of trying to get money is a waste of time for both parties. You need to be focused and directed in your search. In the medical nonprofit example, a well-matched sponsor can underwrite specific equipment, putting their name on everything. Aligning the goals from the beginning ensures that both your organization and your sponsor can create a long-term relationship. As another example, consider the office supply company that partners with an organization whose mission is to combat underfunded school districts by supplying backpacks full of school supplies for children in those districts.

With some creative thought, it becomes apparent that there are many different ways that various sponsors can logically contribute to your cause. Don't overlook them!

Your Volunteers

Of course in your evaluation about adding an event, you'll need to look at the effects on the organization – the pros and cons. The pros, of course, are increasing visibility, hopefully broadening your donor base, and increasing revenues and sponsorships. And of course, the cons are increases in costs, increases in time commitments, and possibly an increase in staffing, even including hiring an additional person to oversee the new event. All these issues tend to collide at one point called "volunteers."

Volunteers are tremendously important to the success of a nonprofit event. Without them, so much doesn't happen. The questions always start with, "How many will we need?" Let me state right now: Sometimes more is not better.

While an organization never wants to turn people away, any volunteer must be precisely matched to the task. In other words, you cannot have a shy, quiet introvert meeting and greeting guests at registration. That immediately sends the wrong message to guests and would make the volunteer shy away (no pun intended) from helping your organization in the future… and they may possess the very skills you could use. In this case, just not at the registration table. There you'll need someone who's engaging, excited, and willing to speak with guests and answer questions so that guests start out at the event feeling positive and excited to be there. Your introverted volunteer may be great at tracking details behind the scenes.

Yes, you'll very likely need volunteers; however, your nonprofit needs someone on staff with strong organizational skills to be able to achieve the positive results you want to generate from your event. Otherwise, you're going to waste an awful lot of time chasing your proverbial tail. In this case, I'm referring to actually training volunteers. Yes, you'll need to train them because an improperly trained volunteer only serves to frustrate attendees. Frustrated attendees do not make an event successful. By training, I mean doing so ahead of time – perhaps walking them through the venue, explaining how the evening/event will progress, making them aware of names of guests they should know, covering housekeeping details like the location of restrooms and the bar. You want every volunteer to be able to answer the sorts of questions

> **Match the volunteer's skill to the right task.**

that any and every guest may ask. You certainly don't want guests going on a wild goose chase looking for things or being met with a volunteer who says, "Well I don't know. I'll find out." You never want that to be the answer, no matter how helpful it may seem.

Strong volunteers can ultimately become strong employees. You never know where your next enthusiastic hire may come from. Additionally, volunteers bring friends... sometimes, a lot of friends. Ultimately, those friends may also turn into donors either with their time and energy or their money or both. Your volunteers already have a shared interest in your mission. They may have started investing in your organization by way of a donation and now desire to become even more involved. Plus, their friends may also become involved either as attendees or through their donations.

Never underestimate or forget how important volunteers are to your success – both the success of a specific event and your overall success throughout the year.

Rock Your Event:

- Your nonprofit is a *business*, and you must make money to carry out your mission!

- Never take your donor base for granted. Know your donors and *why* they support you.
- Donors can often communicate the message of your organization with more impact than you can.
- Maintain your donor base by establishing and nurturing your relationships with them.
- Sponsorships can underwrite the entire cost of an event, so ticket proceeds and other revenue generated goes even further.
- As with individual donors, you need to nurture the relationships you create with sponsors. Never simply take the check and run.
- The greater the sponsorship contribution, the more TLC the company will need.
- Target sponsors that naturally align with your mission in some way.
- Almost every event needs volunteers to be successful; however, more is not always better.
- Match the skill and personality of the volunteer to the right task.

- Good volunteers can turn into great employees.

E: Evaluate

Chapter Two:

V: Venue and Value

Venue and value really go hand in hand… two sides of the same coin, you might say. When you're creating an event, your venue has tremendous value, and that value goes well beyond the amount you'll pay. My guess is that you're wondering why and how these two elements – venue and value – fit together.

The truth is that the venue actually helps set the tone for your event long before the event date arrives on your calendar and before the first guest even walks through the door.

Your chosen venue must be someplace that is memorable and exciting enough – in and of itself – to attract guests who are outside of your regular base. A creative and exciting venue may be enough to make someone who's barely (if ever) heard of your organization want to attend! These are the folks who are going to ultimately increase your donor data base and revenue down the road for your nonprofit.

Even for your regular donors and supporters, an exciting and different venue will help generate greater attendance. If you have an annual fundraiser that you always hold at the same place, you will invariably have donors who start to think, "Been there, done that; I'll just send a check." While a check is nice, nothing beats the having a well-attended event. Don't assume that just because donors have attended in the past that they'll do so again in the future. Keep them interested in your organization with an exciting venue!

Your venue must be memorable… so much so that when it's over, people will say, "We went. It was gorgeous (or fun or exciting or unique – insert the modifier you want), and we thoroughly enjoyed being there!" And they'll repeat this to everyone they know.

Of course, as a nonprofit, you want a venue that is cost effective. However, when an organization gets ready to make a decision on where their event should be held, the decision often and quickly becomes an emotional one. Somebody knows somebody, and it's, "We want to hold it there because she's a nice gal or he's a nice guy or they're a large donor or…." Yes, you cannot discount those factors and they will figure into things, but let me restate what I said at the beginning of this chapter:

The truth is that the venue actually helps set the tone for your event long before the event date arrives on your calendar and before the first guest even walks through the door.

26

Yes, sometimes it is very difficult to find a venue that fits your budget and is approved by everyone involved. My advice is to put your thinking cap on before you simply follow the path of least resistance and "same old, same old."

Make 'Em Special

Everyone likes to feel special, and what better way to make your attendees feel special than to give them "restricted access"? Everyone wants to be in an elite group, and your choice of venue can make that happen.

Look for a venue that is not accessible to everyone. Look for a venue that attendees might not be able to see otherwise. For example, maybe you hold your event at a museum that's closed after hours

> **We all want to feel like we're part of an elite group. Offer that to make your event memorable... and successful!**

and as part of the event, attendees get a behind-the-scenes tour – getting to see parts of the building to which they'd never have access if they were to stroll through the front door during regular hours. How cool would that be?

Or consider a theater, especially for organizations that are involved in the performing arts. You could actually host the event on the stage. Not many people actually get to be on the stage of a large theater. It's unique. They'll feel special.

Another big attraction is always going to be sports teams. Imagine having your event include a tour of the team's locker room or training facilities in the off season. With that choice, you'll probably end up with a waiting list of people who want to attend rather than begging folks to buy tickets.

Now, most of these types of operations are generally quite restrictive and, in many cases, don't open up their facilities for events. However, it never hurts to ask. Talk to them and explain why and how your two organizations can benefit by such an affiliation. You might be surprised!

Creating a Unique Experience

You also want to consider the avenue of creating a very unique experience for your guests. Something they'll get to do that otherwise might not be possible. For example, if your event involves raising funds or awareness for animals, have the event at the facility where the animals are! Your guests will get the chance to interact with those animals. Perhaps you can get into a zoo or aquarium after hours and maybe even have the opportunity to feed the animals. That would be really neat... really different... really memorable.

In the case in which the facility isn't so great as a venue – think animal rescue, kennel, a lot of barking dogs – perhaps you can arrange to bring the animals to the venue instead. Yes, you'll need to get permission and there may even be a security deposit required, but it's all part of creating an experience, not just an event. You want participants to walk away from the event saying, "Wow, that was really, really amazing."

It makes your organization memorable, and attendees will be far more likely to respond when you issue an "ask."

Another avenue for your venue consideration is to create something special out of nothing. Think: warehouses, old armories, or factories no longer used for their intended purpose or otherwise vacant. Reaching new people with this approach is pretty exciting as these can lend

Yes, you can actually make something out of nothing.

themselves to wild design ideas and all sorts of creative, cool stuff... making it fun and memorable! Keep in mind that this type of venue must be easily accessible and that you may need to provide additional help for people with disabilities so that every attendee can have access to the facility. With that in place, the sky's the limit for creating an incredible experience.

Another interesting aspect of selecting a venue could be its "funkiness." Perhaps an odd sort of museum that's not at all mainstream... one people wouldn't think about visiting on their own but will be interested in attending not just to support your organization but to see someplace off the beaten path that they would otherwise never visit.

Start brainstorming about the venues in your geographic location and remember that it doesn't have to be right in your own backyard.

New Faces

To boost value, your event needs to be exciting enough to attract new faces – those outside your current base. Why? The more people you attract, the more money you will generate and the more new donors you can add who will make future donations beyond simply purchasing the event ticket.

A unique venue will be just the ticket to do that. You can get people thinking, "That sounds cool. I don't know much (or anything!) about this organization, but I want to see that place. It sounds fun." And voila, not only do you give new faces a cool and unique experience, you now have the chance to interact with them personally, describing your organization, your mission and purpose, and why they should care and support you.

Isn't that the very point of the event in the first place? Think about places you never thought of going!

The Food

How are you going to feed all of the people who are coming to your event? That's always a primary question and concern.

Your chosen venue may have additional charges, and we'll dive deeper into those shortly.

While unusual venues create really unique experiences, they may also create some logistical issues. One of the first things to consider (especially if you're using a wide open venue, for example a warehouse or armory) is access to kitchen facilities.

Some venues have dedicated catering companies, and by dedicated, I mean: *no other catering companies allowed*. It may also mean that no one, including the hosting organization, is permitted to bring food in from the outside. With this situation, you must use the venue's catering company or perhaps select from their specified list if they happen to use more than one.

That may not be a bad thing. If you're hosting a high-end event, and the catering company is comfortable with and experienced with high-end events, you're golden. However, the opposite can turn out to be true, and that's *not* a good thing. Let's consider the stadium or sports arena again as an example. Here, typically customers/attendees are in the venue to watch a sporting event, and high-end food is not a priority for the customers, so it's not a priority for the venue. They may not have the capability and facilities to serve up the menu you're envisioning. When you mix up a high-end event with "low-end" food, that rarely leads to a positive outcome.

> **The quality of the food must match the quality of the event. Period.**

Other things to think about regarding the kitchen facilities and the catering company: How are they serving the food? Think: china, glassware, silverware. You must know if those items exist at the venue, and if not, whether or not the catering company supplies them. Some do; some don't. If not, there are companies that will rent what you need. The point is that you must read and understand the contract, so you know what is included and what you'll have to rent and provide. It's very important to understand this because, I find, this is generally where the nonprofit tends to lose money. The facility costs, catering costs, shipping/loading costs can combine to push the cost of hosting the event beyond the revenue generated by ticket sales.

Sponsorships can and should help you cover some of the additional expenses as we already covered in the Evaluate chapter.

The Drinks

Fundraising events generally include alcoholic beverages, and this is another area where you'll need to pay close attention. If someone or another company donated wine for your event, will the catering company charge a corkage fee? In other words, a cost not only to bring it to the facility but to serve it to guests as well. And is that corkage fee per bottle or is there a flat fee that covers it all? If you're bringing in spirits, there may be additional charges for those as well.

Always check with the facility and/or catering company about what is allowed and exactly what the charges will be. Do not assign a rookie to review and sign that contract! You definitely want to have someone who understands how contracts work *read through every single line of that contract* so there is clear understanding about every single charge.

Other Logistics

When you venture outside of an ordinary venue like a banquet hall or similar, there may be load in and load out costs. These are effectively charges to get your supplies into the venue and back out when it's over. Be sure to ask if these charges exist and who's responsible. You? The catering company?

These costs can include something as seemingly small as requiring a particular person/staff to carry boxes of equipment, your programs, decorations, etc. Due to liability issues, oftentimes, a venue will not allow you or anyone in your organization to do such a thing.

These costs can add up, so do your homework.

But… don't hit the panic button at the thought of load in/load out costs at an unusual venue and fall back to the ho-hum, same old banquet hall. Oftentimes, it's possible to have some of these charges either fully or partially waived in exchange for publicity for the venue and their promotion in your advertising.

In a convention center or similar venue for your nonprofit event, there can also be charges for seemingly trivial things. These types of charges aren't only found in unusual venues. Even for tasks as simple as plugging in an extension cord, you may not be permitted to do that. Venue staff is required to handle the task, and there could be a fee. Again, read and understand what the contract entails, no matter which venue you choose.

It's not unusual for you to have things that are required to be shipped to the venue in advance. It could be programs, displays, decorations, etc. There may be charges for the venue to accept them (similar to load in costs) in addition to the actual cost of the shipping. As shipping costs are driven by weight, with large, bulky, heavy items, you'll have to budget accordingly. Depending on your venue, it will also cost you to have it moved from the loading dock where it was received to the actual space inside the venue that you'll be using.

> **Do your homework and know all costs, but don't let certain fees steer you away from an otherwise perfect venue.**

There are plenty of costs to consider, and as long as you review and understand the contracts and fees, you can position yourself for your event to raise rather than lose money. Again, do your homework.

Parking

It's often the last thing many event coordinators think about in their planning; however, it is the first and last impression your guests will get of your event. It is a very important aspect of a successful event, and it can be challenging. If your guests encounter a parking challenge, they are already going to be unhappy (or at least displeased) before they walk into the venue. When that happens, their overall expectations are somewhat low. Occasionally, that could work in your favor... provided you absolutely blow them away with the quality of your event. Often, that doesn't happen.

The type of parking you offer as well as who pays for it is driven by the type of event you're having. Street parking is okay for casual events, and ditto to the situation in which your guests have to walk through a parking lot to get to the door. With a casual event, guests probably don't spend a lot of time in preparation. However....

> **Don't let your parking plan be an afterthought!**

In the case of a high-value, high-cost ticket event (think black tie, white tie, gala), it is never, never, never okay to subject your guests to this approach to parking. Valet parking is the way to go, and nonprofits typically cover the cost. Valet parking immediately raises the guests' expectations of the event... before they walk through the door. It is simply never okay to rely on street parking for this type of event and the type of patrons you want to attend.

Depending on your venue, valet parking may already be in the mix. It only becomes a challenge when you need to find a company to handle it and determine how – and how much – they will be paid. A number of different companies that offer this service have very creative approaches to allow nonprofits to pay for the service. Sometimes, the charge is per car; sometimes, there's a flat hourly rate; sometimes a combination, depending on the company.

If the parking is far from the venue, that's a whole 'nuther talk show. The solution is a shuttle; however, the shuttle issue gets to be very, very expensive in a hurry. If you need shuttles, you'll need to determine the type. For example, at a casual event like a golf outing or an outdoor auto show, your shuttles could be as basic as school busses, and your patrons would be just fine with that approach.

As the cost of your ticket price goes up, so should the quality of the shuttle service you provide. Gala patrons are not interested in riding a school bus to the venue no matter how cool and creative that venue may be!

If it will be self-parking in a parking area, the lot should be finished and paved. If that isn't possible, you should provide covered walkways, so guests aren't walking through dust and mud. Your guests may *not* mind (depending on the type of event), but think how impressed they'll be to see you've provided cleaner access. Also, don't assume that because you wouldn't mind walking through a field or unpaved lot to get to the event that your guests won't either. Often, they will. And what's worse: They may not voice it immediately but will be grumbling about it long after the event is over.

Photography

Photographs are one of the most important parts of your evening or event; however, they're often overlooked until the event is unfolding or at least until the last minute. Don't fall victim to this failure to plan.

The most critical photos are generally taken during a reception and include your board members, major donors, and other VIPs. You should also be getting photos of attendees who are there because they "just bought a ticket." These folks are hugely important to drive your future base, so don't overlook them.

When you invite the press (and the more advance notice they get, the better), they generally arrive with a list of photos they want and need to shoot based on how they plan to cover the story. Do not assume that you know what they want. Additionally, do not leave them on their own to find the people they want and need to shoot. Help them out and handle the introductions. Point them in the right direction. They may have multiple events to cover in a single evening, so their time at each event is critical. If they can't shoot what they need in the first 10 to 15 minutes, they'll probably be out the door, and you've lost your opportunity for coverage.

If you are submitting photos, keep in mind the deadlines for submission. Different media platforms have different requirements, and generally, they are not flexible. A print magazine, for example, may have a two- to three-week window from the date of your event for photo submissions with captions. Conversely, an online magazine might need the photos within 12 to 24 hours of your event. They tend to have a tighter deadline because of the immediacy of their publicizing events. When writing captions, stick to the details and forego any flowery prose. They'll likely edit it out anyway. They want concise and clear descriptions. Clearly identify those in the photo from left to right, and it's your job to get the spelling correct. Deadlines, even for online outlets, are usually hard and fast. Miss the deadline and you're out of luck until the next edition, and if too much time has passed (in the example of a print magazine), your information will be considered "stale" and won't be included at all.

Photographs that are intended for print publications (e.g., newspapers, magazines, etc.) need to be 300 DPI (dots per inch) or larger. (If you are uncertain about that reference, find someone who understands photography resolution.) As I write this, photos shot with a smart phone are generally not clear enough and not of high enough resolution to be suitable for print. If you must use a phone, check the settings to shoot at the highest resolution possible and use an app such as Adobe's Lightroom that will give you much better quality (and iCloud storage on top of that). The higher the photo resolution, the better for printing. Photos that do not have enough resolution will likely be rejected for print – they'll look fuzzy or blurry, and no publication wants to show poor photo quality.

Photos for online use do not require the same high resolution; however, you can always convert a high resolution photo to lower resolution for online reproduction, but going the other way (trying to *increase* the resolution of a low DPI photo) rarely results in an acceptable print-quality photo. The issue with photos shot with a phone tends to be insufficient lighting, especially in darker venues. The best approach is to shoot the highest quality and highest DPI you can to meet the needs of the media and press submissions. Even if you try to correct a poor photo in Photoshop or similar software, the chance of rejection is high.

There's more to a good photo than high resolution, even for those that will appear online or viewed via screen versus print. Poorly lit subjects and poorly composed photos will not represent your organization very well, so do not even consider submitting them in the first place.

How do you overcome these challenges? Hire a professional photographer. More often than not, they are worth every single penny and then some. They understand lighting, resolution, and most importantly, the best compositions to make the event and the guests really shine. They have a trained eye and know exactly what to look for. They have better composition skills and where to place people to get the perfect shot rather than a boring, ho-hum, seen-it-all-before photo. Plus, they can get in and out in a short amount of time. They can shoot a reception and the awards portion of the evening and be out the door within about an hour or so. It's money well spent.

Your professional photographer also understands all those pesky resolution details to get photos of your event ready for submission. Additionally, they'll likely be very familiar with the specific deadlines for your local media, knowing when and how to submit.

If you rely on volunteers, that can be a scary prospect. They tend to be inconsistent and get involved with other details of the event, missing important photo opportunities. Most volunteers don't know what to look for and don't know what makes an interesting photo... let alone getting the lighting and resolution correct. The scariest thing you can hear from a volunteer or someone on your committee is, "I know someone who photographs weddings. They'll be just fine for our event." Don't bet on it. Do your homework and hire the right professional.

Another consideration when it comes to photographing your guests is whether or not you have their permission. A professional will generally ask politely to ensure smiles and a nice shot. That polite request, however, is often not enough. It's always a good idea to have some sort of written disclaimer regarding your right to post photos of the event without written permission of the subjects. This information can be along the lines of: "Due to the nature of this public event, your photograph may be taken. ABC Organization reserves the right to post any pictures taken during events on its websites and in other communication without asking permission of each individual in the pictures. (Discretion will be applied, where appropriate.)" This information should be posted on your website page and in signage at the event, perhaps even on the tickets. I encourage you to consult with your organization's attorney regarding the exact verbiage and where/how the information should be posted and communicated. In this age of selfies, it's easy for bystanders to be captured in the background, and they may prefer their image not be posted. Every state is different. Ask your attorney!

Keep in mind that every photo taken during the event can have a long shelf life and be used in the future. Photographs are the way your organization reaches people. They need to be compelling in addition to being correctly focused, properly lit, and clean. Are you willing to risk your large fundraising event to a volunteer who doesn't shoot professionally? Even someone who may take incredible vacation photos may not do a great job indoors with people and using a flash. Volunteers are wonderful; however, they are typically not the right solution when it comes to photographing your event!

Need Jazzing Up?

It's not uncommon for events, especially annual and traditional ones, to get to the point where they feel "tired." It's the same old, same old... "we do this every year" type of thinking. Now it needs zip and some jazzing up.

Here's an example: a polo event that has been running for over 35 years. Yes, it's a tradition; yes, everyone expects it. But even so, you run the risk of even the most faithful patrons not to worry about skipping a year because they can always return next year. How can you jazz that up? Think about adding a classic car show or a symphony or other live music in conjunction with the event. In this case, the venue is determined by the main event – polo, so, of course, it's in a polo field, so you have to take that into consideration because you can't change the venue.

You can't change the venue, but you can add to it, providing extra value to your guests. In this case, add the car show or live music or perhaps a vendor shopping area, meet the players, meet the ponies, etc. That's kind of cool. You can mix it up and jazz it up without changing the venue or the main, traditional event.

In this example, it needed to be jazzed up to attract the younger set who didn't really know about polo. When the movie, *Pretty Woman*,

Perhaps you can't change the venue, but you can always boost value by adding extras.

starring Richard Gere and Julia Roberts, came out, polo events sprang up all over the country. Everybody wanted to do a polo event. It became a long-standing tradition, but now it faces an audience too young to even be familiar with the movie.

The same issue works in reverse as well. What is successful with millennials may not attract those who are over 35. Event planners and organizers have to be very cognizant of the generational issue. While millennials tend to want hip and trendy types of events, typically the real money (in terms of sponsorships) doesn't gravitate toward hip and trendy, particularly in the nonprofit world. It's a balancing act... and you definitely have to find that balance!

Value

Let's take a minute to chat about value. And when I say "value," I'm also including perceived value.

To better understand perceived value, consider a black tie gala. Guests are paying several hundred dollars or more for their ticket, and there is no valet service. The nonprofit or organization *thinks* the parking deck will be just fine. Valet service is going to cost extra, so they don't want to do it. However, the guests think: "What? How can this possibly be? You have a high-end event and you don't offer valet service? What's with that?"

You're off on the wrong foot before they walk through the door!

The higher the ticket cost, the higher the expectation of the event. The dressier the event is, the higher the expectation is also. A higher ticket price demands better food, better wine/spirits, better atmosphere. All of these things are tremendously important in the eyes of the organizer, but they are even more important in the eyes of the attendees. They have set their expectation based on the price of their ticket. This is critical to remember in the early planning stages. Planning a high-ticket event? Then plan on better... everything!

Another aspect of perceived value comes into play with room rental. The venue may trade the cost of room rental for publicity and exposure. If that's the case, the organizer must ensure that the venue's logo/tag line, etc. is on

Ticket price always drives expectation. Be certain perceived value lives up to that.

everything they send out – emails, social media posts, snail mail, advertising, etc., so the venue doesn't feel like it's being taken advantage of. The venue can be added as a sponsor at the appropriate level with the perks associated with that sponsorship cost. For example, if the venue would cost you $5,000, the venue gets $5,000 in perks and advertising to offset the room rental fee. This can ease the nonprofit's burden and make everyone happy all the way around. Sponsorship perks go a long way to offset costs.

Speaking of perks, an organization can offer complimentary tickets to those involved with the venue, like the general manager, sales staff, and anyone who is not working the event itself. This can generate a tremendous amount of goodwill along with including the venue as a sponsor on every bit of pre-event publicity as well as at-event publicity (programs, signage, electronic presentations, etc.). Consider introducing the venue principal(s) and have them say a few words about why they're supporting your organization.

There may not be a way around room rental, so you're faced with an important decision: Is the venue worth the cost and the attraction or not?

The venue is worth the cost if it sets up the tone and conveys the excitement of the event long before the event begins. In other words, it's an exciting place to be and people hear about it on your save-the-date communications. "We're going to be at <insert cool venue here>, so save the date!" People will immediately connect with that and decide right then and there that they want to attend. Then you create event buzz by working with the venue to provide a sneak peek of the event to come!

Rock Your Event:

- The venue sets the tone for the event long before the date arrives.
- Provide a creative venue and unique experience to make guests feel special.
- Create an experience, not just an event.

- You can attract new faces simply by your choice of venue. They are the people who can become future donors.
- Food is an important part of any event. Ensure the quality and presentation of food matches expectation. A high-end event with low-end food is never a good combination.
- Be certain you understand any and all corkage fees.
- Read contracts carefully and be aware of additional costs (e.g., load in/load out, etc.) that will impact the overall cost of the event.
- The type of parking your provide must match the level of the event. No street parking for galas!
- Don't settle for same old, same old… even with annual, traditional events. Figure out how to add value if you can't change the venue.
- Attendees set their expectation based on the price of their ticket.

V: Venue and Value

Chapter Three:

E: Enthusiasm and Effort

Enthusiasm, effort, and extraordinary people. Enthusiasm can make or break an event. You probably already know that. The truth is simple: If your staff is on board with what you want your event to accomplish, the event will be a rousing success. There will be some minor details that may fall through the cracks, but overall, with staff enthusiasm, your event is going to be a complete success!

As an event planner, development director, or executive director, keeping your team on the same page is absolutely vital. However, you must avoid thinking your own ideas are the best ideas or, worse, the only ideas. Every single idea, no matter how silly or far-fetched it seems, should be examined from different angles and perspectives. This is the basis of great brainstorming. The person suggesting the idea should be given the chance to air their thoughts about the benefit of the idea and how they think it could be executed. You never know when an idea is going to come out of left field – and it could be fantastic – but you need to give that employee/staffer/volunteer the chance to present their idea and pitch it to everyone involved.

There are really two benefits to this approach. The first positive effect is the person/staffer/volunteer now feels more a part of the team. They offered a suggestion and had a chance to see what everyone else thought. Even if the idea is not adopted or implemented, you now have *greater buy-in for the event* as a whole because there is a greater sense of teamwork and inclusion. Secondarily, even the wackiest idea can evolve and be morphed into something really great. The initial idea might not be implementable or even acceptable, but it may just spur further creative thinking from the rest of the group that would have never occurred without the initial wacky idea. Again, brainstorming 101 stuff.

Once you have a list of ideas, including every aspect of putting on an event (venue, food and drinks, entertainment, etc.), you must evaluate each idea

Enthusiasm = Buy-in;

Buy-in = Success

from various angles. First and foremost, determine if it will provide a monetary return. Nobody sets out to lose money, but without the right assessment at the start, it happens. An idea also needs to have value, especially perceived value as we covered in the last chapter.

There are other considerations that may, or may not, be completely quantifiable:

- Will the event elevate our brand?
- Will the event increase our donor base?
- Will the event increase our sponsorships?
- What effect will the event have on future donations?

All of these things need to be evaluated for each idea. This sort of review also helps increase staff/volunteer buy-in since you are evaluating ideas based on these defined metrics. The person whose idea gets tossed out is less likely to lose their enthusiasm when they see that the idea wouldn't pay off… literally. And let me repeat: *Enthusiasm will make or break your event.*

Board Members

One of the things most overlooked in event planning is the involvement of board members. Like staff, you need them to be enthusiastic and sign onto the event because you actually need them from the word "go." Board members can and should be responsible for everything from buying tickets, to encouraging others to buy tickets, to getting the word out, to bringing in sponsorship opportunities –

whether the board members themselves become sponsors or have connections who could be sponsors.

Most board members, no matter the type of organization, are in that position because of their background... and the connections they have. They should want to enthusiastically reach out to these connections for various levels of support for the event. They can use their connections to attract additional sponsors as well as additional revenue. Even if it's an in-kind donation, it matters because it will affect how much money the event generates whether it's direct revenue or offsetting of costs.

> **Board members typically have contacts that can boost revenue or offset costs.**

Getting your executive director on board (if that person is not immediately involved in the event planning anyway) is crucially important. You want this person to be a very active participant in fundraising, meetings, meeting potential sponsors, reaching out to the community, and generally being the spokesperson and the face of the organization. I've actually found a lot of executive directors don't like to do that. They like to remain quietly behind the scenes. This isn't necessarily a bad thing; however, if this is case, someone needs to step up and be the face of the organization. Maybe it's the operating director/manager or another management-level person. Donors and supporters – and prospective donors and supporters – support a cause and the people who make the mission happen. That doesn't occur if the organization seems, well, faceless.

Your team will respond better when there is hierarchical buy-in and leadership. You don't want any sort of fire drill in planning and executing your event. Chaos quells enthusiasm. You want things to be organized from the top down with a leader who is setting the example by being involved and getting the whole team excited and enthusiastic about what the event is going to be and how the event is going to benefit the organization and further the mission.

Promotional Efforts

It's not uncommon that once the ball gets rolling, everyone is excited and ready to go, and they start posting all over social media about the event. That's a wonderful thing… until it's not.

The one thing that needs to happen, probably more specifically than anything else, with PR and media is that one person should be designated as the go-to for all social media posts and other media contact. No doubt the organization has its own page/presence on various social media platforms. Depending on how the administration of that is set up, you may already have it restricted to a single person. If not, now is a good time to do so regarding the event promotion. (You may still have others sharing day-to-day/non-event-related information.)

One person (with input from others as desired) should organize the message, create the hashtags, and coordinate all of the other details going forward to make the event a success. *A consistent message through the media is one of the most important things that you can do to make your event a success!* Having one person at the helm for promotion tends to drive consistency. Share this person's contact information with other traditional media sources. The local paper or broadcast station is more likely to share

Promotion works best when the message is consistent!

your story when you make it easy for them to do so. They're busy people too, and if they have to bounce from one person to another trying to get the information, they're less likely to run the story.

Of course, you want everyone in the organization to be sharing event information on their own social media sites. But you want that information, and even imagery, to be consistent. Your staff, volunteers, and board members may be even more inclined to share if you literally give them the copy or graphic to post. "Here's what to say; here's what you should share."

With social media comes hashtags. Again, consistency is key, including hashtags that go out to guests at the event to use. Designate a hashtag for everyone to use (e.g., #eveningatthemuseum). The hashtag must be embraced by your organization, and strongly encourage your attendees to use it as well. Remember: the purpose of the hashtag is to drive people to everything that happened at a specific time. You can have a few different ones, but don't go crazy by having dozens, or you are watering down your efforts and results. Don't make yourself the little fish in a big pond. Too many hashtags will do just that.

Social media is also the vehicle to attract the younger set, either within your organization or as attendees. They not only embrace social media, they live by it. Social media has the potential to spread the word far and wide without *direct expense*. Yup, social media is great; don't ignore it. However, that being said, social media is not the end-all/be-all to promoting your event for a successful outcome.

Social media and how to use it effectively is such a huge topic, I've included a bonus chapter at the end dedicated solely to this topic.

The truth is that conventional support – conventional media support – for an organization is hugely important. Conventional monetary support for an organization rarely comes through social media. Yes, that may change, but at this point, for serious sponsorship opportunities, more traditional media must be embraced as well. Too many organizations today overlook this… completely. Everyone is involved with social media – Facebook, Twitter, Instagram, Tumblr, and everything else out there, and that takes up so much

> **Never overlook traditional media. It is often a greater source of monetary support than social media.**

time that traditional forms of media are ignored. And if you noticed when I referred to the cost of social media, I said it did not incur "direct expense." But it's far from free. The real cost of social media comes in the form of time spent.

Traditional local magazines, for example, can be an effective way to reach potential attendees because they are generally read more than once and shared. A wonderful way to get your message out is to place that message where people are continually looking... and then passing around, sharing with other people. More eyeballs seeing your information with no additional effort on your part. Very cool. There is another aspect to traditional media that has a less tangible yet very real payoff. For example, you send a press release about your event to the local paper and have a conversation with the journalist writing the story. You've started a relationship, and the journalist now has a contact. When a story breaks in the future that falls within your wheelhouse and area of expertise, who will they call? You. Because they already know you. And you and your organization will be cited in the story, getting further publicity. Let me further explain. Let's say your nonprofit serves the homeless. You send the press release about your annual gala. The paper runs the story, with, if you're lucky, an additional interview from you or your designated promotions manager. Great. Winter sets in and dropping temperatures create a crisis for the homeless. The paper wants to run an in-depth story about it. Ah-ha. You're the contact. The journalist will likely call you to get statistics and additional information about how your organization is serving the community during the winter. More people learn about you. Always a good thing.

Another traditional media format is billboards. Billboards are remarkably effective in reaching masses of people who may not otherwise know anything about your event through social media. Those folks can drive by the same billboard every day for a month, seeing your advertisement every single day, every time they drive by. It's a very, very effective way to reach large numbers of people. When you talk to a media company that specializes in billboards, there are a number of different levels of exposure for which you can contract. And electronic billboards are making that easier and easier. Messages can rotate and repeat with a few keystrokes. Remember the cardinal rule about any advertising: One exposure never works; people need to see something about seven times in order to remember it.

> **Direct mail is effective. It's tangible and it stands out in the mailbox.**

That said, digital media, by its nature, will not necessarily remain with the reader the same way. Enter direct mail. How many times during the course of the day do you pick up a card or letter and look at it? Especially a post card. Perhaps you receive a post card promoting an event, and put it on your desk, thinking, "Yup. I'll come back to this later." You'll look at it repeatedly and will continue to do so until you make a decision. Sometimes it, "Well, the event's over and I missed it." But sometimes it's, "Okay, that's over. I'm so glad I went. I had a great time and will certainly be on the lookout for another one."

The advent of social media pushed direct mail to the back burner for a lot of folks. But now with everyone's email inbox overloaded, showing up in a traditional mailbox is a great way to stand out. Companies like Vistaprint® make creating and ordering printed promotional materials reasonably easy, and it's a very cost-effective way to put your event directly in the hands of a potential attendee – literally. Again, enthusiasm is really needed to chase down the various traditional avenues for promotion.

Digital Advertising

In addition to organic posting on social media, digital advertising is also another avenue for promotion. The organic approach (e.g., you, staff, volunteers, board members posting on their own pages to promote the event) is a wonderful way to reach people who already have an interest in your organization. Others can also search for organizations that support certain causes. So if there's someone who's interested in saving the spotted owl, they can find a page that communicates *"This organization saves the spotted owl."* While that's fine to reach a national or far-reaching audience, those people are probably not the folks who are going to attend your event.

You'll have to do a lot more social media posting, including boosting posts or running ads (particularly on Facebook), to generate a lot more actual engagement with your base. Yes, you can target ads geographically, but it takes time, energy, effort, and money. Sometimes, social media is not the best return on your advertising investment.

Another form of digital advertising comes in the form of email, so let's take a minute to talk about that. Yes, I already said (and you already know) email inboxes are overflowing. However, email is a tremendously important way to keep in touch with your donor base, but you have to do it correctly. The worst way to use email is to consistently ask for money. Too many organizations use this approach, and the result is the same. The recipient sees that email and their first thought is, "Oh my gosh. They are asking me for more money ***again***. That's the only reason they reach out. I can't donate anymore. I don't want to donate anymore. I'm irritated. They ask too often."

Unfortunately, many organizations don't email until they need money. They only email to look for dollars, telling people they're looking for dollars because they need dollars, and it irritates their donor base. It is ineffective messaging. It becomes like the boy who cried wolf. When they actually email to promote an event, the message is probably overlooked with the recipient presuming it's another ask... or the recipient has already unsubscribed from future emails and never sees it in the first place.

The better and far more effective approach is to use email to give people information about the organization and mission – information in which they'll be interested. This goes back to what I said earlier about putting a face on the organization. It may seem trivial, but it is hugely important. For example, you could

> **Email is very effective... but only when it's done correctly.**

send an email highlighting one of your board members or a volunteer. "Hey, have you met Jane Doe? She's an awesome person. She's enthusiastic and very passionate about our mission. Here's why she got involved in the first place…." Very rarely will you find a board member or volunteer who's unwilling to talk about the organization. More likely, you'll have to edit and trim what they have to say instead. They're involved because they're passionate. Or you can highlight a story about how someone benefited from the organization. The list for email topics – other than asking for money – is limitless.

Capture the enthusiasm and communicate it. This sort of information makes a huge difference. It gives the reader/supporter/potential donor a nice, warm feeling. Again, it puts a face on the nonprofit. It is an endless and often un-tapped source of talking points that you can share with your base, and it's a way to attract new faces.

In wrapping up this chapter, remember: the key is to *generate and maintain enthusiasm*. With enthusiasm, the efforts always seem easier!

Rock Your Event:

- If your staff is onboard, your event will be a success. Garnering enthusiasm increases buy-in.
- Brainstorm ideas and never disregard any of them.
- Measure ideas against defined metrics.

- Board members (and the executive director, if not already involved) must be included in the planning.
- Promotional messaging must be consistent. Consistent messaging is a component of a successful event.
- A point person should be assigned to manage promotional efforts.
- Leverage social media, but never overlook traditional media outlets. They are equally, sometimes even more, important.
- Traditional media contacts often lead to future coverage for your organization.
- Figure out the ROI for digital advertising. It may not be a bargain.
- Email is very effective, but only when used correctly.

E: Enthusiasm and Effort

Chapter Four:

N: Numbers

Numbers, numbers, numbers. "Everybody loves numbers," said no one ever. But truthfully, the numbers are what it's all about in the nonprofit world – whether you reached your goals, whether you exceeded goals, whether you brought in more sponsors and donors, and so on. The numbers are really what it's all about, whether it's your reach, your revenue, or both. Regardless, numbers make the world go 'round.

Too many times, nonprofits fail to capitalize on the numbers for their event. When the event is over, the statistics are gone or shoved in a drawer and forgotten. Or worse: there is no metric tracking established in the first place... no record-keeping, no evaluation, no nothin'. The event comes up every year, and they do what they always did. And that, in and of itself, is a crying shame. You wouldn't think it happens, but it does all too frequently.

When it's time to start planning the following year and the event is ready to launch, no one has any idea of what really worked in the past, other than going on a hunch. "Everyone seemed to like it, so it must have made us money." Without specifics and measured metrics, you have no accurate idea about what is really going on… and what truly contributed to the organization. I've seen this quite a bit with event planners who exclusively want to handle the event, with all phone calls, emails, and communication going solely to them, handling all advertising, etc. Now when that person leaves – quits, moves to a new position, or departs for any possible reason – the organization is left completely in the dark with no idea of what is actually going on with the event. Honestly, I've seen it happen quite a lot.

If you have an event planner, development director, executive director, etc. who is not tracking sales (or if they have limited sales tracking experience), they won't have a clue as to what works and what doesn't work. They must be able to answer the critical question: "Where do we need to direct or re-direct our funds to be more successful?" And you must also clearly define what constitutes success in the first place – a revenue goal, profit goal, expanded reach, improved attendance, or some combination of those things. Without those answers,

> **Numbers are really the foundation of any event, so it's crazy, if not catastrophic, to overlook them!**

organizations typically get to the event's conclusion wondering why they lost money or why their sales are down from previous years.

Let's take another look at event planners who exclusively want to use one form of advertising over another to drive ticket sales. For example, you have an event planner who exclusively wants to use social media. "Social media is where it's at; it's where our market is. Everyone is on social media." And so on. Inevitably, for an organization that takes this route – solely relying on social media as their main driving force for ticket sales – sales will decline. In some cases, they will plummet compared to traditional forms of advertising.

Toss traditional media aside, and suddenly you'll find that donors who have been involved and who have supported the event and organization are cast aside, overlooked, or completely forgotten. While social media is fun, it is also ever changing. It is simply not the panacea for any event planner. Social media will not resurrect a failing event or an event that is woefully mismanaged. Yes, it may change in the future… but you must always have the metrics in place to measure the social media impact and prove that it works! Ah, numbers!

Creating "Fiefdoms"

Another consideration when it comes to handling events with event planners or even some development directors is the creation of "fiefdoms." In other words, the individual who is responsible for the event is so intent on controlling every piece of information regarding it that they take on the role of feudal lord. If something happens to that person, all of the details are completely lost. No one ever thinks it can happen... until it does. Not only is that poor planning, it prevents any succession planning as well.

> **One person and _only one person_ knowing all of the details is a recipe for problems if not disaster.**

With people and development directors who take this approach, not only is there an attitude of "This will never happen to me," there is also an attitude that total control equates to job security. "Everyone has to come to me," they think. "I'm the one with all the answers, so it makes me very important – indispensable, even."

What this approach really does is ensure that the event will never get better. It will never get bigger. It will never grow in reach in terms of incoming donors or new guests or sponsors. With the feudal lord approach, the bigger, better ideas never come to fruition unless this individual creates them. "Don't worry; I've got this," they say. Yeah, right. Until they don't. Until it's too late and the event falters or falls apart completely. Trust me. It happens far more frequently than you can imagine.

What really then happens is the remaining people are left to try to organize the event and pull it off on the fly. Of course, that rarely has a positive outcome, and the stress level leaves everyone with the "Well, let's just get through this at all costs and figure it out later" attitude. Later… after the event is over and the books are covered in red ink.

It may seem like I've gone off on a bit of a rabbit trail to cover this topic in the "Numbers" chapter, but the point is that no one person should *ever* be fully entrusted with all of the planning and organization. Numbers make or break any event, and more than one person should have input and be aware of what's going on.

Cost Calculation Checklist

To help you keep tabs on all of your costs (and we covered many different cost factors in the "Venue and Value" chapter), I've developed this checklist for you to use. (Plus you'll find the full version in the Resource section at the end.)

- ❑ Venue
- ❑ Insurance
- ❑ Catering
- ❑ Corkage fees
- ❑ Equipment rental
- ❑ Load in/load out charges
- ❑ Shipping/receiving
- ❑ Parking
- ❑ Music/entertainment
- ❑ AV equipment rental
- ❑ Advertising
- ❑ Programs/printed materials
- ❑ Decorations

Ticket Strategy

In talking about numbers, we must address ticket strategy as ticketing is a revenue driver. For the love of God, stop the two-for-one promotions. Let me say that again: Stop the two-for-one promotions! The only caveat to that is if you are looking to increase attendance for an event, then this approach can work... for one, single year. After that, this strategy must stop. Otherwise, you are simply conditioning your audience to look for promotional prices, and you will never sell a full price ticket to your events again.

By repeating the two-for-one promotion every year, your guests will expect it, making a price increase nearly impossible to execute.

I have worked with organizations that, over the span of ten years, never increased their ticket prices. Ten years! Think about that. How many things have you attended in your life where the ticket price remained the same for ten years? Your costs have increased, so if your prices have stayed the same, it makes no sense. It is certainly not a sound business strategy, and you're setting yourself up for loss.

If you want your VIP tickets to be $250.00 for example, add value rather than reduce price. Every single time you send an email, emphasize what is included in the price of the ticket, effectively selling that ticket continually. Two-for-one

Costs go up, so ticket prices should go up as well.

promotion? You're cutting the revenue you can generate in half yet keeping the value the same. No business operates that way. You shouldn't either.

I also recommend to my nonprofit clients that they never... ever... use a commercial organization for ticket sales that will not share the list of purchasers. Of course you want that information! It only makes sense, yet there are many organizations that use these services on the promise of a huge reach and increased ticket sales only to be left in the dark after the event with no idea who purchased tickets. So much for expanding reach and trying to expand the donor base. In truth, you have the right to know who purchased tickets along with their contact information. Your list is your commodity. It has enormous value, and it will have considerable impact moving forward after the event.

Beware that these companies also take a significant percentage of your set ticket price – sometimes as much as 50 percent or even more. In return, they claim they'll generate more ticket sales for you, but that is often not the case. You may be stuck seeing the margin on each ticket at five to ten dollars, barely covering the cost of having the guest attend the event. Pile that on to the nonprofit scrambling after the event and dedicating hours upon hours trying to determine who attended (having purchased a ticket through a service) to maintain future contact and you've created a recipe for disaster.

Good luck trying to find these people or identifying them during the event. And even if you are successful, they're not going to want to give up contact information to gain access to the venue. A guest who buys a ticket through a discounted service generally will not become a repeat attendee or donor. They're there for the party. They're not really there for the organization and its mission, which is fine, if that's what you're interested in doing. Keep in mind with this approach that you create hardship for yourself to attract future donations. Most nonprofits want to have people attend who are interested in their mission and will continue to support the organization either through repeat attendance, future donations, or ideally, both.

Forecasting your ticketing strategy and establishing a plan for ticket promotions is very important. If you're constantly in the promotion mode, people get fatigued. They'll stop paying attention to social media posts, the post cards you mail, and the emails you send. They think they've already seen it all and that everything is on sale all the time. This is very similar to retailers who constantly send 20-percent-off coupons. They've conditioned their audience to expect them, and those folks will never buy at full retail again.

Guest and donor fatigue is very really. People get tired of seeing all that information, so they ignore it and stay home. Never assume that your past attendees are sitting on the edge of their seats just waiting for your email that going to include the next big promotional deal for your event. These days, there is so much information about so many events that your marketing and ticket promotions need to be precise and targeted, so you're not exhausting your audience. Just because the event is first and foremost in your mind doesn't mean the same is true for your donor base and prospective attendees.

Ticket sale timing is everything. The timeframe for invitations has gone from a short six to eight weeks for paper invitations to a minimum of eight to ten weeks. The save-the-date cards are going out anywhere from three to four months in advance to as much as six months ahead of the event. Again, be very targeted and specific with your marketing and information, and don't overwhelm your audience. Price the event at what it's worth. Do a *rare* promotion and sit back and watch ticket sales rise because you've added value and made it worth it.

Debriefing

If you've ever had the misfortune of going through the scenario I described earlier in this chapter (i.e., a single person with all of the details who departs) or survived an event that was a disaster for any reason, you know the common reaction: "Let's get this behind us" along with the desperation to forget about the whole thing.

Worst. Possible. Approach. EVER.

You must absolutely have an in-depth debriefing meeting… and yes, sometimes it's appropriate to refer to it as a post-mortem, especially if the event lost money. You must take a hard look at every aspect of the event and evaluate each one. Of course, the only way you can honestly and accurately evaluate is with numbers! And you won't have the right numbers if you don't have the metrics in place at the start in order to be able to measure.

Attendance is always important and easy to measure. But could the attendance have been better? How many people were turned away because the venue was sold out? Did anyone

> **Win, lose, or draw, you should hold a debriefing after every event to evaluate each and every aspect.**

keep track of that? But isn't "sold out" a good thing, you ask? Perhaps, or perhaps it's time to look for a new venue that can accommodate even more guests. Ah… a good topic for the post-event debriefing and a place to start for planning next year's event for greater success.

How much was spent on advertising? What was the ROI? In other words, how well did the advertising pay off? This can always be a challenging metric, so you must – from the very beginning – develop a way to measure. Sometimes, it's a matter of asking how attendees found out about the event. A survey is a good approach. Sure, not everyone will take the time to answer, but getting some input is far better than guessing. Surveys can be done via email after the event (or even before, perhaps during registration) or by way of a simple form distributed at the event. Maybe even have volunteers conduct a fun man-on-the-street sort of approach during the event while handing out tickets for a prize drawing to those who answer.

"How did you find out about it?" is really a critical question that can drive the advertising choices for the next event. Yes, maybe a lot of people did learn about it through social media, but you'll never know unless you ask!

Revenue, like attendance, can be pretty black-and-white: total sales/auction income, etc. less all your expenses. However, take the time to really drill into all of the expenses to get a far clearer picture of success. "How much did we pay for swag bags? Were they appreciated and did they make a difference or would anyone even notice if we didn't hand them out next year?" Again, in order to effectively evaluate, you have to have the metrics in place from the start. You should certainly have a way to account for all the various expense categories – food/beverage, venue, advertising, decorations, etc.

Finally, in your debriefing, you must also consider staffing… and not just the servers, bartenders, etc. at the event. How well was the planning staffed? It is all too common for nonprofits to be woefully understaffed for event planning and execution. Understaffing only compounds the problem of an event that is not going well in the first place. You end up with desperation and the "let's just get through this" attitude with the belief that you can make it up on the next event. That never happens, and the cycle starts all over again. Stress continues to rise. Good employees and volunteers start heading for the exits.

It's always sad to see organizations go through this. If they only understood how important the numbers and the metrics actually are, they would be so much better off!

Credit Cards

As we've been discussing numbers, it's the ideal time to also talk about credit card use for payments to your organization. Plastic is pervasive, and people expect to be able to use credit cards. Period. Yes, there are fees to your organization for giving them that privilege, but those fees are simply "the cost of doing business" and far better to pay a fee than to have a potential attendee or donor forego buying a ticket or making a donation because they cannot do so with a credit card.

The most important thing to address in talking about credit cards is the way in which you collect the data. Far too many organizations are quite haphazard about the way they handle credit card numbers and information. Without a doubt, right now there is a nonprofit someplace that is sending out forms, instructing donors or event guests to fill out their credit card information, sign it, and mail it back to the office. "We'll take care of processing your payment," they say, thinking they're making it easy. What could possibly go wrong with that? Right?

> **Collecting credit card data via hard copy forms? Stop immediately!**

The truth is that this is one of the leading ways that credit card information is stolen when dealing with a nonprofit. If this is your way of doing business via credit cards, that practice has to come to a stop. Immediately. No more sending out forms or including them in printed newsletters and other hard copy forms of communication. Seriously, stop now.

I am not overstating the danger of collecting credit card information in this fashion! I cannot think of any approach that is more unsafe than putting credit card information in the mail, hoping it reaches the nonprofit, and then hoping the staff doesn't leave the form lying around for anyone to see. The same thing is true regarding taking credit card information over the phone. The same pitfalls exist.

"But our staff is trustworthy," you protest.

I say, "Don't take the chance... ever!" Stop now or you are opening up your organization to countless things that can go wrong even to the point of ending up in court facing a lawsuit. Do not be casual with this information, and don't wait for one of your donors to complain and point out the dangers of this practice to you.

Instead, encourage donors and guests to pay via check or use an online portal to register for the event and pay with a credit card via a secure site.

Certainly, in the early days of the internet, there were plenty of folks who absolutely would not enter credit card information online. Website security has come a long way, but you must ensure that your online collection of credit card data is secure! Or you're no better off and in the same boat as you were with the fill-out-your-credit-card-number-on-this-form approach.

Additionally, there are a number of different services that will handle credit card processing for nonprofits and their events. Do some research to determine the best approach for your organization. You'll need a payment processing tool that is secure and completes the backend operations, taking funds from your donors' accounts and placing them into yours. There are literally hundreds of them. Do your homework.

Be sure to research the fees. Different providers have different fees for providing credit card processing. Some get very expensive. Some may have a transaction fee of $.99 per transaction plus a $2.00 ticketing fee. Occasionally, you'll see one that has a $1.00 ticketing fee plus credit card transaction fees. Lest we forget, those transaction fees typically run from 2.5 to 5.5 percent (sometimes more) depending on the type of credit card.

Run the numbers. The lower transaction fee may or *may not* be the best deal. Be certain you are evaluating all of the costs and variables. Here's an example of what I mean: American Express tends to have higher fees, meaning less money for the nonprofit. That said, don't be too quick to decide you won't accept American Express. The flip side is that studies and statistics show that those who use American Express credit cards tend to donate more than those who use other types of cards. Ah, an important variable to consider. Run the numbers!

Most ticketing platforms will require you to accept VISA, MasterCard, American Express, and Discover as a group on their platforms. Overall, that's not a bad way to go about it, and the costs tend to even out and be somewhere in the center around 3.5 to 4 percent. That's not bad.

So, now that you've done away with hard copy forms to collect credit card information (you have eliminated those, right?), you must monitor activity – as it is occurring, no matter if you've chosen PayPal or any other platform. When I say "monitor," I don't mean taking a look at the conclusion of the event to see what happened. I mean pay attention every day to the amount of money that is going into your account.

That money is the lifeblood of a successful event, and those numbers need to be accurate. Every day, you should verify that what is said to be going into your account is actually going into your account. I've seen far too many organizations fail to do this daily check (or turn it over to someone else to handle) only to be faced with an accounting nightmare – or a loss – after the event concludes.

The most important thing I can impart about credit cards is really security. When your guests respond to your invitation and pay with a credit card, they expect that you are going to guard their information. It's an implied covenant. The minute there is some sort of breach or an unexpected charge on their account, they're going to be unhappy… with you. It's never enough to place the blame on the credit card company or processor. Should a particular situation arise, you or the event planner must be on top of it the minute it happens. Failure to do so reflects poorly on your organization, and now you have a guest who will never return and never convert into an ongoing donor.

In doing away with those dangerous hard copy forms, be ready for some push back. Undoubtedly, there are going to be guests or donors who have consistently written their numbers on the forms and mailed them back, and they may not be happy about not being able to pay that way any longer. Most people are "change resistant"! Now it's your job to let these particular guests or donors know that the change in the process is for their own best interest and security – protecting them from a dangerous situation that could open up their credit card to fraudulent charges. You never want that to happen because that's a surefire way to lose guests and donors!

In closing this chapter, if you weren't a "numbers" person before you started reading it, I doubt I've converted you into someone who now loves numbers. But I certainly hope I've impressed upon you just how important they are not only to a successful event but to a nonprofit that is thriving rather than simply hanging on and surviving.

Rock Your Event:

- Fail to embrace the importance of numbers and you'll doom your event from the very first meeting.
- You must have metrics in place from the outset of your planning, so you can measure the effectiveness and success of every facet of your event.
- Without knowing the ROI on each component of your event, you won't really know what worked and what didn't – critical information for the success of your *next* event.
- Avoid allowing anyone to create the dreaded event "fiefdom" in which only that one person is controlling everything and only that one person knows the numbers.

- Avoid the two-for-one ticket sales. They effectively cut your revenue in half.
- Never use a service for ticketing that will not share the list of purchasers along with their contact information.
- Hold a debriefing session after every single event – especially those that may be losers – to avoid repeating mistakes.
- In this day and age, you must accept credit cards as payment. In this day and age, you absolutely cannot gather credit card information via hard copy forms.
- Do your homework and plenty of research in choosing your credit card processing platform. Remember, the lowest transaction fee may not necessarily be the best choice. There are many variables to consider.

Chapter Five:

T: Time

Time. We all could use more of it, especially when it comes to event planning. To have a successful event, time management is a crucial element. Everyone involved is busy and often busy with other day-to-day operational tasks needed to keep the organization running. Layer on event planning and execution, and the stress level goes up – way up.

I emphasized earlier about the importance of having a single person responsible for promotions. True. However, when it comes to overall planning, communication and shared information are critical. (Even your promotions person has to share what they're doing!) Event planning must be collaborative. When information resides with only one person, it quickly breeds frustration with the rest of the staff. They're not happy. They can't get the information they need to execute the tasks assigned to them. If you bring them into the process and utilize their time effectively and successfully, your event – from the first meeting to the conclusion and post-event debriefing – is going to run like clockwork, no pun intended.

First things first: When you know your event date, work backward for every other task. This is the heart of all project planning. There needs to be extraordinary attention to detail with a constant eye on the calendar to ensure that deadlines are consistently met. That said, you (or whoever is in charge) may or may not be the right person to handle the task of staying on track. Perhaps someone on the staff or committee who revels in details should be assigned to maintaining the to-do list and calendar.

No matter who takes charge of this, a calendar or spreadsheet of some sort is needed from day one of event planning, beginning with the first meeting and listing the goals of things to be accomplished and the deadline for each of those goals. Here's what I mean when I suggest you work things backward. Take event programs, for example. Determine when you actually need them in hand. If you are transporting them to the event, at the very least you need them the day before. If you need to ship them to the event, you'll need them sooner to allow for transit time. Once you've determined the date they're needed, next determine how long the printer will need to produce them. Prior to handing the project over to the printer, you'll need to know how long the graphic artist needs to create the layout. With that date in mind, now you'll know when all the copy (perhaps order of events, sponsor names, etc., depending on what information you include) must be finalized. Ah, now we're really working backward. Put each of these dates and deadlines on your spreadsheet.

Sponsorship packets are another example. First determine a deadline for sponsorship sales to close, keeping in mind that you must allow time for any promotion that is part of your sponsorship packet. (No sponsor will be happy if they only receive promotion a day or so prior to the event.) Then determine how long that sales window will be… six weeks? Eight weeks? Longer? When you know that date, now you know when the sponsorship packets must be ready for distribution so sales can begin. Then you can continue working backward regarding printing, layout, copy, etc. similar to the program example.

These details and dates add up fast, so you must have a way to keep track of them all. A spreadsheet, like Trello, Smartsheet, Slack, etc., provides you with a starting point and end point… and can be shared to keep everyone on the same page. Everyone can see where various tasks are in terms of development and meeting deadlines and can update information as needed. No matter what tool you choose, you must organize these details. It makes the process easier and reduces quite a lot of stress among staff and volunteers when they are able to see all of the tasks for which they're responsible and the specific deadlines they need to meet.

There are countless different types of software and programs to facilitate the process. Yes, you can create your own spreadsheet/timeline (known as a Gantt chart in the project planning world), but it may be well worth it to invest in more specialized software

> **Stress can quickly quell enthusiasm for the event. Get organized to reduce stress.**

to handle this aspect of planning your event – especially if event planning happens frequently (or even annually) in your organization. Once you find an app or software you like, grab it, use it, and stick with it! One constant source of frustration for staff is a constant change of direction and constant change in the way you account for things. Find one method. Keep it. Use it. Use it a lot. There may be a learning curve for certain software programs for everyone involved, so don't keep re-inventing the wheel. It ultimately saves time (once you and your staff have mastered the learning curve) and reduces a tremendous amount of stress for everyone involved in the organization and the event.

Deadlines Approaching!

As the event date on the calendar gets closer and closer, the amount of time consumed in tending to the details and to ensure deadlines are met becomes enormous! Know this in advance and accept this fact. Allow extra time on your calendar (ditto for staff/volunteers) for this. Nothing adds stress like trying to juggle too many things at once. In the days and few weeks leading up to the event, block out even more time than you think you need for event prep. Don't allow other projects to creep in, and in the last days, even some daily tasks will have to wait or be delegated to someone else, so you can dedicate all of your time to event details and tasks.

Once you've planned and directed an event, you'll certainly have a better sense of how much time is needed for various tasks. Sometimes, entire days can be spent working on things that are incredibly intricate but that you might think can be done quickly. Seating charts and place cards are a prime example. These can take a tremendous amount of time, and their execution is critically important. Seating may seem like a simple thing, but you really need to get it right. You have sponsors. You have high-profile donors. You have guests who are new to the organization who have no affiliation at this point other than "they bought a ticket." Each of these attendees must be handled accordingly and in the order of importance for which they want to be recognized. (Note that I said "*they* want to be recognized." Be certain that you are clear about this. Some folks, even some of your highest-level donors, may want to keep a low profile. Honor their wishes.) It is extremely important to address all of these factors when creating your seating chart to ensure you have a clear, concise plan… and one that makes everyone happy. I assure you: this is not accomplished with a snap of your fingers.

How will you name your tables? What are you going to do with particular people who are not speaking to one another? Seems petty, yes, but it happens all the time, and it matters. It becomes very challenging to put everybody in a seat – in the right seat. You wouldn't think it would be a major challenge, but get this wrong and it can really put a damper on the event and derail every other detail to which you've paid such close attention. It takes a tremendous amount of time. Plan for it and allow time from the start for these sorts of details.

Registration Time

The next consideration regarding time at your event is the method by which you'll handle registration. Will you have a registration table, where every guest walks up to check in and get their table assignment and other information (e.g., program, name badge, etc.)? This can quickly lead to queues forming... with guests spending their time waiting in line. You can alleviate the bottleneck with multiple tables, proper signage, and staff or volunteers providing welcome and direction. Or will you use place cards in a reception area where guests will find their name and table assignment and then find their table among the sea of tables in the ballroom? Your choice, of course, depends on your specific event and venue. Gala versus more casual sort of thing.

With technology, one of the tricks I've discovered is the ability to text table numbers to each guest. It saves a tremendous amount of time when they arrive to check in because they already know where they're going to be seated. It also makes it easier on your folks, who are usually seated at the registration table, sorting through various papers to find everyone's seat assignment. In this scenario, all guests need to do is "check in" at the registration table. They already know their table assignment. It saves a tremendous amount of time for your staff, but more importantly, for your guests. They don't want to waste time standing in line at registration. Whatever you can do to streamline that process will be well received!

In this day and age of online ticketing and order placement, it is very easy to leverage technology to register your guests electronically. Many software packages provide this capability. You can actually stand at the doorway with an armada of staff and volunteers with iPads or tablets who can check each guest in very, very quickly and efficiently, especially if you've already told them prior to the event where they'll be seated. Picture it: You greet them, check them off, someone hands them a program, and off they go to enjoy the event, and it may have taken all of 10 seconds. That paints a nicer picture than a long line of guests waiting at a registration table.

Embrace technology to expedite the registration process. Your guests want to get through the door and start having fun rather than waiting in line.

For a very large event, you can use scanning capability (or hire a company that provides it), and you can have guests through the door in fewer than two seconds. That's all it takes to scan a ticket and get them into the event. The technology is already available for nonprofits to use what sports venues and arenas have been using for years. Don't be afraid to use technology to save time as you're getting people into your event. You want to make it easy and efficient, and your guests will be much happier getting into the event and having fun than standing in line waiting for you to check them in.

Auction Time

Also be certain that you are leveraging technology for fundraising auctions that are often a part of events. There are plenty of different companies that enable you to hold your auctions online, making it easy for guests to bid all the way through the event… which is kind of cool. However, the less cool flip side is that you'll have guests on their phones looking at and bidding on auction items to the possible exclusion of conversation with others at the table or paying attention to special speakers, presentations, etc. That is something to consider and decide: "Do we go ahead and put it online and have people be able to use that capability to view and bid while seated at dinner… or do we stop the auction beforehand… or do we run a silent auction online before the event actually starts?" There are a number of approaches and all can work.

A word about online auctions: Most people do not bid in an online auction in the run-up to the event, provided the auction continues at the event. Instead, they'll wait for the event to see the items in person and then develop their strategy about how they're going to bid once they're at the event. It's rare to see someone actually place a bid in an online auction when they are going to be at the event in person. That's something to keep in mind in your planning.

> **Consider various methods for conducting an auction and what will work best for your event.**

On the other hand, online auctions can be a tremendous way to reach out to greater numbers of people. You can reach folks (who may or may not be attending the event) with emails that announce the online auction in the first place with subsequent emails telling recipients when new items have been added. It's very exciting and a great way to build some buzz. "Click here to see what is now available and start bidding!" Don't be afraid to put auction items online and share the information. People will make the choice when it hits their inbox whether or not they want to look, but leave that choice up to them. Don't assume that because you are tired of seeing the items it means your guests are tired of seeing them as well.

A quick word about online auctions: Be sure to use a tried-and-true app/software, and it's not a bad idea to do a test run with a small online auction before and completely separate from your main event. Do your homework and talk with other organizations that have used your chosen or preferred software regarding any problems or glitches they encountered.

In discussing auctions, I want to segue for a few paragraphs to talk about the auctioneer. Too often, I've seen organizations seek out a volunteer, board member, or someone on staff to handle the auctioneering duties. Unless this chosen person is a professional auctioneer, I say don't do it. Non-professionals who are really good at live auctions are so rare as to almost be non-existent. Usually, the microphone is turned over to someone who should never have a mic in the first place.

There is a real art to driving a successful auction. Yes, your staff or volunteer may have all the passion in the world about raising money for your mission, but that passion rarely converts to driving energy in the room… and driving energy also drives bidding. Driving bids converts to more dollars! If you use someone without auctioneering experience, the auction tends to be flat and items sell for considerably less than they should. Bring in (and yes, pay for) a professional auctioneer who knows how to get the audience excited, how to get them involved, and how to drive a bit of competition among bidders, and your chance of success in terms of raising more money escalates.

For example, let's say one of the auction items is a trip to California or another hot destination. Your volunteer auctioneer may be too busy with other event details to really do their homework and understand **and promote** the value of the trip package during the event – the accommodations, airline carrier, amenities, points of interest, etc.

A good auctioneer will be prepared, can talk about the item, and knows how to comment to get the audience wound up as the event progresses. They may also be able to provide some guidance to you before the event regarding your items, their value, and the diversity of the items on the auction block. Trust me, you aren't the first nonprofit to hold a fundraising auction. Your chosen professional has probably done countless events and knows what generates bidding and what does not. Generally, you do not want more than a handful of live auction items, or attendees may get quickly bored and stop paying attention to the auctioneer and what's going on. Lack of attention will also cause an auction to fall flat. A few spectacular offerings are better than several ordinary ones.

So back to our discussion about the impact of your guests' time. Remember that long line we talked about regarding registration? Well, it's even worse when it comes to checkout for a silent or live auction. Everyone has been at the event for a number of hours. They've had food. They've had wine or drinks. By now, three or four hours have passed. It's been fun. But they're ready to call it a night and go home. They get to the auction checkout area, and the line is miles long, moving incredibly slowly. For each checkout, some volunteer needs to run around, find the item, get it to the desk, etc. The winner has to provide credit card information and staff has to process it. It certainly puts a damper on the fun and isn't a great way to end your event. Again, in this situation, you are wasting your guests' time.

Instead, so much of this can now be done online. You can use programs such as Square, Stripe, PayPal, etc. to expedite checkout, either for silent or live auctions. Consider using an auction service as they'll have capabilities to checkout in seconds because they've collected credit card information at the start or prior to the event. Auction winners can be out the door in 30 seconds – a much more positive memory about the conclusion of the event.

Do some homework and research. Various approaches change your level of control of the process. You have to decide the best approach for your organization. The bottom line is to be able to get your guests and their items out the door as fast as possible at the conclusion. If they want to stick around and continue interacting, great. However, if they're ready to get on their way, you want to be able to allow them to do so.

Keep in mind that your goal with event registration and auction activity and checkout is to move your guests from arrival to departure as quickly as possible, so they can fully enjoy and appreciate what happens in the middle – your message and all the fun activities. It's incredibly important that these details are taken into consideration very early in the planning process. Do not think you can figure it out the day of the event! You will not be able to so and the result is chaotic disaster, leaving your guests frustrated and far less likely to attend your next event.

Time – time to plan, time to execute, and saving time (both yours and your guests') – is a critical component of any successful event!

Rock Your Event:

- Start with your event date and work every task backward to establish your deadlines.

- Find a planning software program or app that works well for your organization. Use it and stick with it.

- Block plenty of time for event-related activity on your own calendar with more time allotted as you near the date.

- Many tasks (like seating charts) are critically important and take more time than you may imagine. Don't rush these details. Allow plenty of time for them.

- Determine the most efficient way to handle registration, so you aren't creating long lines and wasting your guests' time. Don't be afraid to embrace technology to expedite the process.

- If your event involves an auction (silent, live, or a combination), consider the pros and cons of online bidding and determine what makes the most sense for your event and organization.

- Use a professional auctioneer. The higher bids they can generate almost always offset their fee.
- Auction checkout lines are tedious and a bad way to end your event. Put technology to work, so you can get folks out the door when your event is over.

Bonus Chapter:

Making the Most of Social Media

Social media is so pervasive that by its very nature it can be exhausting. And it can get tiresome pretty fast.

In formulating your social media campaign for an event, there are so many different elements that must be considered. Which social media platforms will we use? Who's going to post? How often are we going to post? Are we going to pay to boost a post or run Facebook or LinkedIn ads? If so, how often and what's the budget? Which posts will we boost and who decides that? Honestly, I could go on, but you get the point. These questions can be endless.

When you first start a campaign, everyone in the organization needs to understand who is responsible for posting on all of the different media platforms. Once that happens, everything can be funneled through one person, so it makes it a lot easier to keep track of what's being posted and who is engaging with your audience. We already covered the concept of a single person and single point of contact for promotions in Chapter 3: "Enthusiasm and Effort." Again, consistency of your message (including social media postings) leads to a successful event. With a "single person" approach to promotion and social media, you create the consistency you need.

Social media can be a full-time job in your organization, not just when it comes to event planning and promotion. It takes time to understand the best approach, execute it (e.g., dropping pixels into events), and then tracking all of the analytics from Google Analytics and Facebook (just to name two) to determine the extent of your reach for the event, how your social media presence is boosting your website, and if you are spending money in the right places to benefit your organization. Oftentimes, because of the nature of easy payments for online ads and post boosting, it becomes very, very easy to spend an incredible amount of money on social media without getting any real tangible returns. Or without getting *measurable* returns. Return on social media investment can be very difficult to measure. Many times, the "return" on your social media investment is soft. That is, it generates awareness but doesn't generate donations – or at least measurable donations unless you really take steps to funnel and track donations through social media. That's very worthwhile but also wildly time consuming. Many organizations quickly become very frustrated with the entire process involving social media.

Despite the frustration, never neglect social media. It can kick your event into high gear, especially during the event. With smart phones, everyone these days is always walking around with a camera and a video recorder. Most everyone likes to post on their social media accounts, and everyone likes to see pictures of themselves. Establish your event hashtag (e.g., #ThisEventIsFabulous) and be sure to encourage your guests to use it when posting during (and after) your event. Use signage with the hashtag at the event and include it in your program. Be certain to mention it in opening remarks. Really encourage hashtag use.

With this approach, ultimately your goal is to Google your hashtag to be able to see everything that anyone posted online – photos, videos, comments, etc. It's a very effective way to capture the event (time consuming to an extent but effective!) for post-event recaps and stories. Plus it gives you a nearly unending supply of content to share in future social media posts and in your emails, giving you reason to stay in touch with your base. In the photography section of the "Venue and Value" chapter, I covered the importance of using a disclaimer regarding shooting and sharing photographs from your event. Be sure to review that important information and consult with your attorney regarding the exact verbiage to use.

At one of my previous companies, we gave away every single photo we took by making them all available for download on our company website and then communicated that with follow-up emails. The amount of increased traffic to the website was extraordinary. Keep in mind that increased traffic to your site improves your search engine ranking. With improved search engine ranking, when someone searches for an organization that carries out your particular mission, you are going to populate closer to the top (if not at the very top) of the result page. Ah-ha. A new person just found you. Perhaps they'll engage and perhaps they'll become a new donor.

> **People like to see pictures of themselves. Capitalize on this with a hashtag for your event.**

Post-event stories and photos open the door for you to continue posting on social media and continue to engage your base throughout the year. One of the things that turns donors off in a hurry is constantly receiving requests for money. If it doesn't actually turn them off, it does become tiresome, and "donor fatigue" is very real, as you probably already know. Don't add to the problem by only ever reaching out when you need money. Every nonprofit always needs money! Your donors are well aware of it, so be certain your contact with them is not always an "ask." You can quickly lose them – even your long-standing, tried-and-true donors may turn away. You don't want your social media posts to be so focused on the end goal (raising money) that you forget about what matters to start – your donors and their perception of your organization.

Platforms & Choices

Social media is easy enough to do. Most people already have an account or accounts on various platforms. Chances are that if you have a teenager somewhere in your organization, they can get it done in a matter of minutes. Ridiculously fast, sometimes. A quick caveat to follow up: Use that teenager to *teach* you or your designated point person. It's very unlikely you want a teen to be crafting your message!

With your social media pages and your event, the largest amount of time is going to be dedicated to creating content for specific posts, whether it's Instagram, Facebook, Twitter, etc. So which one to use? Before you jump up and decide to use all of them, the first thing to consider is your base and how they use social media. Which platform does the majority of your base use? Where are they hanging out on social media? For example, if you know the majority of your base is on Facebook, that platform should be the focus of your attention. The other thing to consider is to use a social media platform integrator like Hootsuite (or something similar), so you can post simultaneously to various social media platforms at once, effectively sharing the same message across them all.

Social media is a tremendous avenue for you to get your information out. It's also a tremendous consumer of time. It may seem "free," but remember that you are always paying with time – yours or someone else's. Somebody has to be involved with social media (posting, engaging, commenting, etc.) almost all the time in order for it to truly be effective. But it's here to stay, and people are using it.

> **Know your audience. Where are your donors hanging out on social media?**

As I mentioned, everyone with a smart phone is also walking around with not only a camera but a video recorder as well. Enter Facebook Live. (As I write this, Facebook Live is the 800-pound gorilla for social media live streaming. That may change, but for now, I'll refer to Facebook Live.)

It's easy to use Facebook Live to live stream right from your event. Anyone with a Facebook account can do it. It's always fun, and people like to see it. You're capturing the excitement of the event as it's happening. You can also do Facebook Lives leading up to your event, capturing the event prep. "Hey, I'm coming to you live from XYZ Organization, and I just wanted to share these cool items that just arrived that will be featured in our auction." Perhaps you're getting preparations together, staff and volunteers are decorating and setting up the venue, the catering company is putting down tables and tablecloths. All those sorts of things that lead up to the event are going to build excitement for it. Stuff like that. People love it. Even a short segment before a planning meeting. "We're just getting ready to meet about our upcoming Food Festival. We're planning out great activities and have several wonderful restaurants that will be participating this year. It's going to be a wonderful event... and delicious. Be sure to mark your calendar and visit our website for all the details and to get your tickets. You won't want to miss it. Okay, gotta run."

Keep in mind that you are live, so maybe a few practice runs are in order before you actually push the button to start your live stream. Plus, it puts you in front of all those people who are following you, and it may actually be shared by some of them, who will then start to follow you as well. It's a good thing.

There's no limit to the length of time for which you can live stream, but there is certainly a limit to viewers' attention spans. Imagine your nonprofit is hosting a wine tasting or some sort of food festival. Sure, it would be great to focus a Facebook Live on some of the scrumptious tastings, etc. However, there is nothing worse than for someone to tune into your Facebook Live and discover it goes on and on… and on. Be careful. The person handling it may now suddenly find themselves with sort of rock star status, and they're wandering around in a continuous live feed. Actually, most watching will get bored quickly and tune out.

Multiple short live streams are far better than one long one.

Instead, serve up your event in short snippets using Facebook Live. "Hey, I'm here with John and Jane Doe, two of our great supporters. Take a minute to tell our audience your favorite part of the event and why you support us." People are much more inclined to watch short segments of your event, like two-, three-, or four-minute blocks rather than sticking with it for 30 minutes or longer. Another benefit to live streaming in short snippets is that it makes it far easier to repurpose those in the future.

So, yeah, Facebook Live is a great thing. On the other hand, it can be the worst thing, too. Once you go on Facebook Live, it's out there and it stays out there. That may not be a good thing if you have someone who is not particularly comfortable or who freezes up at the idea of being on Facebook Live. That is not going to set the right tone or send the right message about your organization or your event. Make certain that whomever you are going to put in front of the camera is going to be articulate and sharp, on point, and who knows what they're talking about and can add passion to the message. Do as many practice runs as you need to!

Other Considerations

Instagram is also a wonderful way to present your message visually. It is focused on the photography, and you can easily add two or three different hashtags. Add a comment to a great photo along with your hashtags. Imagery with short messages is what Instagram is all about. And it is a great way to reach people who are going to stop and click on a particularly compelling photograph: a beautiful table, wonderful decorations, unique venue… all of those are things that will attract people to your event, and that's exactly what you want.

Twitter started with a limit of 140 characters. Although that restriction is no longer in place, with that as its foundation, a lot of people still use this platform for the briefest bits of information. So think about short messages (e.g., "save the date" or "we just finalized a delicious menu," etc.) and add links to your organization's website or ticket purchase site for more information.

Although there is now quite a lot of crossover, each social media platform still tends to have its original niche (i.e., Instagram for photos, Twitter for short bursts of information, etc.). You can actually repurpose a lot of information between platforms. Photos posted leading up to the event on Instagram can be re-used on Facebook the night of the event in conjunction with a live stream. Be creative and remember that you don't need to start from scratch every time. Re-use content in various ways, in various places, and at various times. You can repeatedly get your message out. All of that matters, and all of that takes a tremendous amount of energy and effort. Find the right enthusiastic person to take the lead, and they can keep your organization and event in the limelight and make rock stars of everyone involved!

Rock Your Event:

- Social media is a great tool for promotion and to get your message out, but it does take a lot of time.
- Remember the importance of message consistency. Ideally, one person should be taking charge of social media.
- Often, social media's ROI is soft: awareness vs. donations.
- Create and promote hashtags for attendees to use when sharing photos of your event. It is the ideal way to capture and conglomerate them.
- Post-event photos provide a wealth of content to remain engaged with your base without always asking for money.
- Determine where your donor base hangs out on social media. That's the platform that should get the majority of your focus and energy.
- Live streaming is ideal to promote your event sharing both preparations and happenings at the event.

Resources:

Here are links to some of the vendors/providers that I referenced in The EVENT Technique. I am not promoting any of these companies or being critical of any that I have not included. My goal with this section is to simply give you a head start on your own research if you need it.

Donor Software:
Blackbaud®
Donor Perfect
Donor Pro
Giftworks/FrontStream

Direct mail/printing:
VistaPrint®
Staples®

Email providers:
Constant Contact®
Mailchimp

Ticketing providers
Blacktie-America
Showclix

Eventbrite
ModTickets

Auction Software
Capterra
BidPal
Silentauctionpro

Seating Chart Software:
Perfecttableplan
Blacktie-America
Socialtables

Collaboration Spreadsheets:
Trello
Smartsheet®
Slack

Payment Portals:
Square
Stripe
PayPal®
1stPayMobile

Others:
Google Analytics
Hootsuite®

Facebook Live

GoingUp

Buffer

Cost Calculation Checklist

❏ **Venue:** Venue is generally the most expensive portion of the event. There can be charges that you may not think about, like the cost of moving chairs and plugging in the electricity. Yes, depending on your location, you can be charged for these things, and they can creep up on you and, before you know it, you've busted your own budget!

❏ **Insurance:** It is an absolute must! Many companies offer event policies at very reasonable rates, and it is worth every penny for the peace of mind that it brings. Do NOT go into an event without insurance. EVER. Generally, a policy with $1 million in coverage per incident is adequate. If you have multiple events in a calendar year, it may make more sense to obtain a policy that will cover them all. Shop around for the best plan for your organization.

❏ **Catering:** This can include a number of different charges including service charges, upcharges for better alcohol, delivery charges, cancellation charges, penalty fees if you don't hit your expected guest count, etc. You MUST read your catering contract very carefully to understand everything that could be a potential charge. For example, never assume that you can bring in donated wine at no charge. Generally, a catering company will charge a corkage fee that can be as much or more than buying the wine from the caterer. Save that donation for another event.

❑ **Liquor license:** In addition to corkage fees, you may need to purchase a temporary liquor license – one permit for a specific date/place. Costs will vary by municipalities.

❑ **Equipment rental:** Chairs, tables, a stage, drape, etc. Depending on your venue, they may provide those, possibly with a load in fee per person. Table cloths, china, stemware, and flatware can be negotiated on a per person basis, so you don't get hit with all of these different charges at once.

❑ **Load in/Load out:** Again, these charges depend on the venue. They represent the fee to allow equipment and supplies to be unloaded at the venue's loading dock. Generally, these occur at convention centers or concert halls on a larger scale. Smaller venues usually do not charge these fees.

❑ **Shipping/receiving:** Similar to load in/load out, some venues charge to receive, store, and retrieve items that you ship in advance. Plus, you have to cover the cost of shipping.

❑ **Parking:** Don't forget parking as it often comes with valet charges or lot fees. These can vary widely, and you must determine in advance if you'll underwrite all or some of the parking or leave it to your guests to find and pay to park. Often, you can negotiate a preferred rate. Search for venues that have a lot or have parking close by and ask for a discounted rate for your guests if you are not underwriting the cost. If parking is far from your venue, you'll have to hire a shuttle service or bus company to move guests from parking to your event and back.

❑ **Music/entertainment:** These costs can skyrocket depending on the number of hours the band is performing and present. Typically, you can have a band before or after dinner and forego live music during dinner, or you can put together a pre-recorded playlist and use the venue's sound system. This saves enormously. However, ensure you are aware of any royalty agreements or copyright infringements regarding using recorded music. You may have to pay a broadcasting fee. Check with your organization's attorney for clarification and details.

❑ **AV equipment rental:** This is another overlooked line item that can cause your costs to blow your budget. Find out first if your venue provides AV equipment and to what extent (e.g., microphone/speakers vs. big-screen projection capabilities). Your needs will depend on your presentations. Try to negotiate or find a company that will donate it for you. It never hurts to ask.

❑ **Advertising:** Depending on the number of events you hold per year, you may be able to negotiate for multiple ads, billboards, commercials, etc. You can control costs by maintaining your brand and the look and feel of the ads from one event to the next.

❑ **Programs/printed materials:** Programs are always a challenge. You want your guests to have the information, but they often don't look at them or leave your well-designed, beautiful programs behind. Guests may glance at them and even carry them home, only to have them hit the recycle bin. Consider emailing attendees after the event, including the program information and thanking them for their attendance. It's another way to promote your sponsors, and it just might spur another donation.

❑ **Decorations:** They can range from simple to incredibly elegant and elaborate... and expensive. The level you choose should always reflect your event. Casual and laid back events don't need that many decorations. For formal dinners or galas, plan accordingly. The higher the ticket price, the more elaborate your decorations must be.

However, deals can be found. Do your research. You may find cool things that look fabulous without breaking your budget.

❑ **Flowers:** You may or may not opt for floral arrangements, depending on your event. While flowers are always beautiful, they can also have powerful aromas that may or may not be welcome. Strongly scented floral centerpieces may overpower the aroma of the meal placed in front of your guests. Use your judgment regarding if and where to use flowers.

About the Author

Jill Kummer is a successful serial entrepreneur and the former owner and president of Blacktie-Pittsburgh, an event support company for nonprofit organizations that provided a "soup-to-nuts" turnkey approach to event planning and execution. During her ownership, the company managed over 1,000 events, including online ticket sales and use of other cutting edge technologies. Blacktie-Pittsburgh photographers took more than 100,000 photographs to enable event hosts to fully leverage content for post-event communications and upcoming event promotions.

With her years of experience in event planning and expertise, Jill is a sought-after consultant for companies and organizations that seek to make their events more productive, efficient, and, most of all, profitable. A graduate of the University of Wisconsin-Stout with a degree in Hotel/Restaurant management, she now lives in Pittsburgh, Pennsylvania with her two dogs, Cocoa and McKenna.

Made in the USA
Monee, IL
02 December 2021

83697658R00075